EVOLVING UNITED STATES GRAND STRATEGY:
HOW ADMINISTRATIONS HAVE APPROACHED
THE NATIONAL SECURITY STRATEGY REPORT

A thesis presented to the Faculty of the U.S. Army
Command and General Staff College in partial
fulfillment of the requirements for the
degree

MASTER OF MILITARY ART AND SCIENCE
Strategy

by

JEFFREY V. GARDNER, MAJ, USA
M.S.I.R, Troy State University, Troy, AL, 2001

Fort Leavenworth, Kansas
2004

MASTER OF MILITARY ART AND SCIENCE

THESIS APPROVAL PAGE

Name of Candidate: Major Jeffrey V. Gardner

Thesis Title: Evolving United States Grand Strategy: How Administrations Have Approached the *National Security Strategy Report*

Approved by:

_____, Thesis Committee Chair
Robert D. Walz, M.A.

_____, Member
Brian D. Allen, M.A.

_____, Member
Stephen D. Coats, Ph.D.

Accepted this 18th day of June 2004 by:

_____, Director, Graduate Degree Programs
Robert F. Baumann, Ph.D.

The opinions and conclusions expressed herein are those of the student author and do not necessarily represent the views of the U.S. Army Command and General Staff College or any other governmental agency. (References to this study should include the foregoing statement.)

ii

ABSTRACT

EVOLVING UNITED STATES GRAND STRATEGY: HOW ADMINISTRATIONS HAVE APPROACHED THE NATIONAL SECURITY STRATEGY REPORT, by MAJ Jeffrey V. Gardner, pages 60.

This study assesses how different US Presidential administrations have approached the national security strategy report. It focuses on the elements of continuity and the elements of change between selected national security strategy reports from the four administrations required to submit this report to Congress. This thesis introduces the purpose and requirements for the national security strategy report. The thesis will also portray the security environment that preceded each national security strategy report and describe the selected reports from 1988, 1991, 1996, and 2002. Then these four selected strategies are analyzed exploring for elements of continuity and elements of change. The criteria for comparison will be requirements of the report required by the 1986 Goldwater-Nichols Department of Defense Reorganization Act and the traditional US foreign policy schools. The thesis concludes that the national interests of the US remain relatively constant; however, different administrations have contrasting objectives and approaches to reach those objectives.

TABLE OF CONTENTS

iv

ACRONYMS

DIME	Diplomatic, Informational, Military, and Economic instruments of national power
DOD	Department of Defense
GWOT	Global War on Terror
NATO	North Atlantic Treaty Organization
NSC	National Security Counsel
NSSR	National Security Strategy Report
WMD	Weapons of Mass Destruction

ILLUSTRATIONS

vii

TABLE

CHAPTER 1.

INTRODUCTION

> For the role of grand strategy--higher strategy--is to coordinate and direct all the resources of a nation, or band of nations, toward the attainment of the political object . . . the goal defined by fundamental policy. (1967, 322)

B. H. Liddell Hart, *Strategy*

Background

A primary responsibility for any President is the protection of the American people and security of the state itself. Grand strategy is the way that the executive branch sets out to attain this end. Presidents are unique, but each one documents his grand strategy into an overarching national security strategy for the United States. Up until 1986, no requirement existed for any grand strategy document, or any real expectation of its contents even if it was written down.

Passed into law in 1986, the Goldwater-Nichols Department of Defense Reorganization Act requires the president to submit an annual *national security strategy report* (NSSR) to Congress outlining the administration's grand strategy. This document is supposed to specify national objectives and the use of all the instruments of national power including diplomatic, military, and economic. This document has significant ramifications for policy formulation and the subsequent actions taken by numerous government agencies. It is intended to drive the development of US foreign policy and national military strategy.

The first NSSR was released in 1987, three months after the Goldwater-Nichols Act became law. Between 1986 and 2002, there have been four different US administrations and major fluctuations in the geostrategic security environment. The

1

international order has transformed significantly over this time. We have gone from the bi-polar Cold War, to the fall of the Berlin Wall and multipolarity, through Desert Storm, to the ethnic conflicts in the Balkans and Africa, and on to the post 11 September world. This research will describe the geostrategic environment during which each NSSR was written and then analyze the contents of each strategy report.

Research Questions

The primary research question this thesis will answer is: How has the NSSR evolved with changing presidential administrations? There are several subordinate questions that also will be examined:

1. What are the major traits and themes within the selected *national security strategy reports*?

2. Do the *national security strategy reports* identify the US National Security interests and objectives and the planned use of the instruments of national power?

3. How do the different National Security Strategies compare and contrast with respect to the traditional schools of thought on foreign policy as defined in *Special Providence* by Walter Russell Mead.

Definitions

Many terms in international relations and national security often have similar meanings. Whenever possible the terms in this thesis will primarily be derived from the Department of Defense (DOD) as specified in Joint Publication 1-02, *DOD Dictionary for Military and Associated Terms*. For the purpose of this study, the following definitions will be used throughout the document.

<u>National Security</u>

National security is an often used term with many meanings. DOD has defined national security simply as: "A collective term encompassing both national defense and foreign relations of the US" (DOD 2003, 357). However, national security is much more complicated as addressed below by former National Security Council staff member Carnes Lord:

> The core areas of national security are foreign affairs, defense, and intelligence, and the most important agencies are those laying claim to primary responsibility for each of them-the State Department, the Defense Department, and the Central Intelligence Agency . . . Beyond these core areas of national security, there is a more or less well-defined periphery which includes international economic policy, certain scientific and technical issues, mobilization and emergency planning, and space policy. (1988, 36)

National security has taken on wider definitions as the world has become more globalized, interconnected, and increasingly threatened by nontraditional entities, such as terrorists and the environment. Regardless of how one chooses to define "national security", the fundamental purpose for this country is derived from US national values.

<u>National Values</u>

National values make up the foundation that national security is built upon. "U.S. national values represent the legal, philosophical and moral basis for continuation of our system. These values provide our sense of national purpose. They can be found in the nation's founding documents such as the Declaration of Independence and the Constitution" (Yarger 1997, 2).

These national values are the starting point for national security and any national strategies or policies.

> National Security Strategy must start with the values that we as a nation prize . . . values such as human dignity, personal freedom, individual rights,

ethical conduct, and the pursuit of happiness, peace, and prosperity. These are the values that lead us to seek a global order that encourages human rights, self-determination, the rule of law, legitimate institutions, economic prosperity, the peaceful settlement of disputes, and the elimination of injustice. The ultimate purpose of our National Security Strategy is to protect and advance those values. (Manwaring et al 2003, 117-118)

National Security Interests

If the national values are the foundation of US national security, then American national interests are the cornerstones. Donald M. Snow defines interests as "the shared goals, deriving from some common political principles, that provide entities some perceived political principles, that provide entities with a perceived political advantage" (1998, 175). Interests are broad aspirations and are often intangible.

U.S. national interests are expressions of U.S. values projected into the international and domestic arenas . . . U.S. values are based on what is esteemed and absolutely essential as the philosophical, legal, and moral basis for the continuation of the U.S. system. These attributes are deeply engrained in our political system and domestic environment . . . . In other words, values are principles that give the U.S. political system and social order their innate character; they provide substance to U.S. culture and create further principles upon which to base national interests. (Sarkesian et al. 2002, 5-7)

The definition of national security interests and examples from the DOD are the "foundations for the development of valid national objectives that define US goals or purposes. National security interests include preserving US political identity, framework, and institutions; fostering economic well-being; and bolstering international order supporting the vital interests of the US and its allies (DOD 2003, 358).

Army *Field Manual 1: The Army* states that national interests are the purpose of the nation established by the constitution. "These broad, enduring national goals are expressed more specifically in terms of national interests, which provide the basis for national security policies" (Department of the Army 2001, 16). The below national

interests have remained fundamentally unchanged since the late 1940s

- To preserve the sovereignty of our Nation, with its values, institutions, and territory intact.
- To protect U.S. citizens at home and abroad.
- To provide for the common welfare and economic prosperity of our Nation and citizens. (Department of the Army 2001, 16)

However, the many authors and the US Army have opined that national interests

have remained relatively unchanged since the end of World War II. These three interests

are essentially: (1) preserving US sovereignty; (2) protecting US values, institutions, and

people; and (3) providing economic prosperity (Department of the Army 2001, 16).

These three interests are evident throughout all four NSSRs analyzed in this research.

Robert Mandel writes in *The Changing Face of National Security*, that the added

national security aspect of a stable world has imbedded itself as a "dominant national

security goal" (1994, 25). He goes on to say, "Stability seems to have become an even

more central security concept in the post-Cold War world, as in a fluid anarchic world

states have more consciously emphasized in economic, political, and Military arenas

status quo ends of national security" (1994, 25).

National Security Objectives and Goals

The terms national security objectives and national security goals are often used

interchangeably. "U.S. national security objectives are broad goals (i.e., ends) refined

from the key national interests. They provide a general guide for strategy in specific

situations, and imply a closely integrated defensive and proactive use of all the elements

of national power" (Manwaring et al. 2003, 119).

The DOD defines national objectives as, "The aims, derived from national goals and interests, toward which a national policy or strategy is directed and efforts and resources of the nation are applied" (DOD 2003, 357). For the purpose of this research, national security goals and national security objectives will be considered synonymous.

<u>Elements and Instruments of National Power</u>

The US armed forces capstone doctrine manual, Joint Publication 1, *Joint Warfare of the Armed Forces of the United States,* succinctly describes the instruments of national power

> The ability of the United States to influence events to its advantage worldwide depends . . . (on) the effectiveness of the Government in employing the instruments of national power. These instruments are diplomatic, economic, informational, and military and are normally coordinated by the appropriate Executive Branch officials often with NSC assistance. They are the tools the United States uses to apply its sources of power; including its human potential, economy, industry, science and technology, academic institutions, geography, and national will. (DOD 2000, 6)

The diplomatic and military instruments of national power are the ancient and clearly understood aspects of a state's power. Economic power is more complex, and involves not just government trade policy and foreign aid, but the sum of a states industry, resources, and even private investments. Joseph Nye of Harvard University states that "economic power has become more important than in the past, both because of the relative increase in the costliness of force and because economic objectives loom large in the values of postindustrial societies" (2002, 8).

Addressing the informational aspect of national power, Joint Publication 1 states, "The informational instrument of national power has a diffuse and complex set of components with no single center of control. In the American culture, information is freely exchanged with minimal government controls (CJSC Joint Publication 1, I-7). This element of power has increased in importance since the advent of the computer, satellite communications, news networks, and the Internet. "The information revolution is making world politics more complex by enabling non-state actors, for better and worse, and reducing control by central governments" (Nye 2003b, 227).

There are a number of references to the instruments of national power as diplomatic, informational, military, and economic often called "DIME." The responsible government agency for each element has been considered the "instrument" of national power. For example, the Department of State is the instrument for the diplomatic element of power. This sounds plain; however Admiral (retired) Henry E. Eccles writes that "these various elements of power cannot be precisely defined, compartmented, or divided, it is normal to expect areas of ambiguity, overlap, and contention about authority among the various elements and members of any government" (Eccles 1979, 70).

There is significant overlap between multiple government organizations, and exclusive responsibility for an element of power by one agency is rare. Additionally, two U.S. Army War College professors wrote "Increasingly, the term 'element of power' is used interchangeably with 'instrument of power' in official publications" (Yarder and Barber 1997, 6). For the purpose of this research, the term instruments of power will be used.

Discerning the Difference Between National Interests, Objectives, and Goals

A close reading of the above definitions reveals may similarities between the relevant national security terms, e.g. interests, objectives, goals, purposes, aims, intents, and aspirations. As Donald Snow points out "the concepts of interest and, more specifically, national interest are both hazy and controversial" (Snow 1998, 175).

Since these key national security terms are ambiguous and often interchangeable, this thesis will use a model that should serve as a more solid framework to examine national security. This model is the ends, ways and means framework of strategy.

Ends, Ways, and Means

General Maxwell D. Taylor was one of the first to characterized strategy as "consisting of objectives, ways and means. We can express the concept as an equation: Strategy equals ends (objectives toward which one strives) plus ways (courses of action) plus means (instruments by which some end can be achieved)" (Lykke 1989, 3). Below is an effective elaboration of these three aspects of ends, ways, and means from the U.S. Army War College.

> Ends (objectives) explain "what" is to be accomplished. Ends are objectives that if accomplished create, or contribute to, the achievement of the desired end state at the level of strategy being analyzed and, ultimately, serve national interests. Ends are expressed with verbs (i.e., deter war, promote regional stability, destroy Iraqi armed forces).
>
> Ways (strategic concepts/courses of action) explain "how" the ends are to be accomplished by the employment of resources. The concept must be explicit enough to provide planning guidance to those who must implement and resource it. Since ways convey action they often have a verb, but ways are statements of "how," not "what" in relation to the objective of a strategy . . .
>
> Means (resources) explain what specific resources are to be used in applying the concepts to accomplish the objectives and use no verb. Means can be tangible or intangible. Examples of tangible means include forces, people, equipment, money, and facilities. Intangible resources include things like "will," courage, or intellect. (Yarder and Barber 1997, 6-7)

Strategy

The term strategy has many diverse meanings and usages. *The Webster's Dictionary* includes elements of planning as well as employment (Morehead 1995, 650). Strategy in general is both a "process and a product" (Marine Corps 1997, 37). This research will only address the product aspect of strategy. Strategy is also closely associated with the military as B.H. Liddell Hart defines strategy as "the art of distributing and applying military means to fulfill the ends of policy. For strategy is concerned not merely with the movement of forces -as its role is often defined- but with the effect" (Hart 1967, 321).

Others have viewed strategy as a primarily foreign policy endeavor. However, Carnes Lord states "A serious strategic planning effort at the national level cannot in any case limit itself to foreign policy narrowly understood. It must encompass elements of military strategy as well as strategic intelligence, and integrate them with the diplomatic and political dimension of national security. In addition, it cannot avoid at least some consideration of economic as well as domestic policy (and political) factors" (Lord 1988, 91).

The broader and modern definition from Colonel Dennis M. Drew and Dr. Donald Snow states that strategy "is a complex decision-making process that connects the ends sought (objectives) with the ways and means of achieving those ends" (Drew, Snow 1988, 13). Since the term "strategy" by itself has many meanings and can be misinterpreted, this study will focus on the phrase "grand strategy".

Grand Strategy

This research will address the national security strategies of the US as the overarching international policies of the state. Another term that represents the plan for overall application of national power to attain desired ends is "grand strategy". "At the highest level, grand strategy is the way a state intends to pursue its national security goals. From this, several other strategies are designed that are focused on specific regions or issues. Thus we have military strategy, economic strategy, political strategy, and psychological strategy. In addition, there are US strategies for the Middle East and other parts of the world" (Sarkesian et al. 2002, 36).

The DOD gives this definition: "national security strategy — The art and science of developing, applying, and coordinating the instruments of national power (diplomatic, economic, military, and informational) to achieve objectives that contribute to national security. Also called national strategy or grand strategy" (DOD 2003, 358).

Assumptions

In order to compare the selected *national security strategy reports*, it is essential that an assumption be made about US foreign policy traditions. There are many historical viewpoints to use in assessing the framework of US foreign and security policy. Of those available, the theories of Walter Russell Mead's four traditional US foreign policy schools outlined in *Special Providence* are most useful to this study for the reasons cited in chapter two.

It is also critical for this study to consider the NSSR itself as the actual strategic vision for the President as the statement of grand strategy. This research will not entertain concepts that the NSSR is a ruse or propaganda. This thesis accepts as fact that the NSSR is the actual vision statement and overall intent of the US President for foreign and security policy.

Scope

This study will focus on national level vision and intent as defined by the *national security strategy report*. This thesis will be a content analysis of selected *national security strategy report*s and not a policy formulation analysis. This study will remain in the unclassified realm, knowing full well that classified *national security strategy report*s and supporting documents exist.

The scope of this research is directed at overarching foreign policy and defense policy, not domestic politics. It is impossible to completely separate any administration's policy from domestic politics in the United States, but that is not the focus of this research. It is also beyond the scope of this study to discuss particular regions where policy is applied, or implementation of these strategies at all.

This study does not have the capacity to compare subordinate policies such as the supporting National Military Strategies. Additionally, this research will end with the September 2002 National Security Strategy report, even if a more recent report is released during the course of the study.

Significance of the Study

There are few studies contrasting the different approaches to the National Security Strategy report. There are numerous works on differing foreign policies and a number of critiques of individual *national security strategy reports*. There are also a many works that propose alternative National Security Strategies. However, there have been no expository comparisons of the existing *national security strategy reports*. This research is intended to fill this gap with an analysis of four selected *national security strategy reports* and the requirements of the Goldwater-Nichols Act. This research will also use the relatively unique device of the four traditional foreign policy schools of Wilsonian, Jeffersonian, Jacksonian, and Hamiltonian. This study will add to the small body of research by giving some frame of reference to the different approaches on the NSSR itself.

11

CHAPTER 2.

RESEARCH METHODOLOGY

Research Design

The purpose of this research project is to examine the progression of the National Security Strategy from Presidents Reagan through George W. Bush. The research design for this study is a descriptive comparative content analysis. The critical element of the methodology is to compare the actual contents of selected *national security strategy reports* themselves. The framework of analysis for comparison will be the requirements of the Goldwater-Nichols Act and the four traditional US foreign policy schools. The intent of this design is to identify differing traits and themes in selected *national security strategy reports*.

In order to accurately describe these strategies, it will be important to set the stage for each report by noting the international security environment of the time for each strategy. Consistency when describing the international security environment will be accomplished by using the *Strategic Survey,* published annually since 1966 by the International Institute for Strategic Studies (IISS). This organization is a non-partisan group based in London who state, "The IISS is independent and it alone decides what activities to conduct. It owes no allegiance to any government, or to any political or other organization" (IISS 2003).

The *Strategic Survey* includes an overview and analysis of the major global political, economic and foreign-policy developments from a non-aligned viewpoint. The *Strategic Survey* will be used for the corresponding year of each NSSR and gives a uniform way to compare security environments.

The thesis will examine one NSSR from each of the four administrations required to submit them. The four National Security Strategy reports of 1988, 1991, 1996, and 2002 were chosen based on the timing of the political environment or events occurring in the international security environment.

The 1988 *National Security Strategy Report* from President Reagan was selected because the first NSSR was released in 1987; only three months after the Goldwater-Nichols Act became law. The 1991 *National Security Strategy Report* from President George H.W. Bush was selected since this immediately followed the first Gulf War, which was a key point in international affairs. The 1991 NSSR was the first to recognize the end of the Cold War and specified a formal departure from a containment strategy to one oriented on regional conflicts (Jordan, Taylor, and Korb 1999, 85).

The 1996 *National Security Strategy Report* from President Clinton was selected because it was from both the post-Somalia and Post-Dayton Peace Accords period. This was another key point in international affairs with relation to international organizations and the role of the United States. President George W. Bush has only released one NSSR to date, the one from September 2002.

Goldwater-Nichols Act Defense Reorganization Act of 1986

When analyzing the separate National Security Strategies, they will be compared to the requirements of the Goldwater-Nichols Act Defense Reorganization Act of 1986. This Act details four explicit requirements of the contents of the *national security strategy report*. This research will specifically address the following two items from the Act below

> (1) The worldwide interests, goals, and objectives of the United States that are vital to the national security of the United States.

13

(3) The proposed short-term and long-term uses of the political, economic, military, and other elements of the national power of the United States to protect or promote the interests and achieve the goals and objectives referred to in paragraph (1). (United States Congress 1986)

<u>Mead's Four Traditional US Foreign Policy Schools</u>

The analysis will next use the four traditional US foreign policy schools of thought as a basis for comparing these strategies. Walter Russell Mead expressed these four schools in his book *Special Providence* as Jeffersonian, Hamiltonian, Wilsonian, and Jacksonian. In Walter Russell Mead's own words, here is a synopsis of the four foreign policy schools:

> The Hamiltonians are people who think the United States needs to become the same kind of great power in the world that Britain was at its peak . . . We should try to build a global order of trade and economic relations that keep us so rich that we can afford to do what Britain used to do, which is to keep any one country from getting too strong in Europe and Asia to affect our vital interest, to threaten us . . . .
>
> Then you've got its opposite, the Jeffersonian view, which says the United States government should not go hand-in-glove with corporations. That will undermine democracy. It'll get us involved with despots abroad. We'll be supporting evil dictators because some American corporation has economic interest that is advanced by this. And, also, this is going to undermine democracy at home . . . a Jeffersonian, who sees the Word Trade Organization (WTO) as a corporate, big-government plot against democracy at home and democracy abroad . . . "If we'd never set foot in the Middle East, we wouldn't have these problems," say Jeffersonians. That's the logic of antiwar movements, and we've certainly seen a lot of Jeffersonian [values] over the generations.
>
> Wilsonians--and I think we all intuitively know what that is--hold the belief in the United Nations, international law. The United States should be pushing our values around the world and turning other countries into democracies whether they like it or not. And the U.S. should also work multilaterally in institutions. We should be supporting things like the International Criminal Court, the Comprehensive Test Ban Treaty. And we should not be unilateralist in our approach. We should put human rights ahead of trade, and so on.
>
> Then finally, you've got a group called the Jacksonians, for Andrew Jackson . . . [The idea is]: "Don't bother with people abroad, unless they bother you. But if they attack you, then do everything you can." . . . when somebody attacks the

hive, you come swarming out of the hive and you sting them to death. And Jacksonians, when it comes to war, don't believe in limited wars . . . . They shouldn't have started the war if they didn't want casualties. (University of California Berkeley 2003, 3-4)

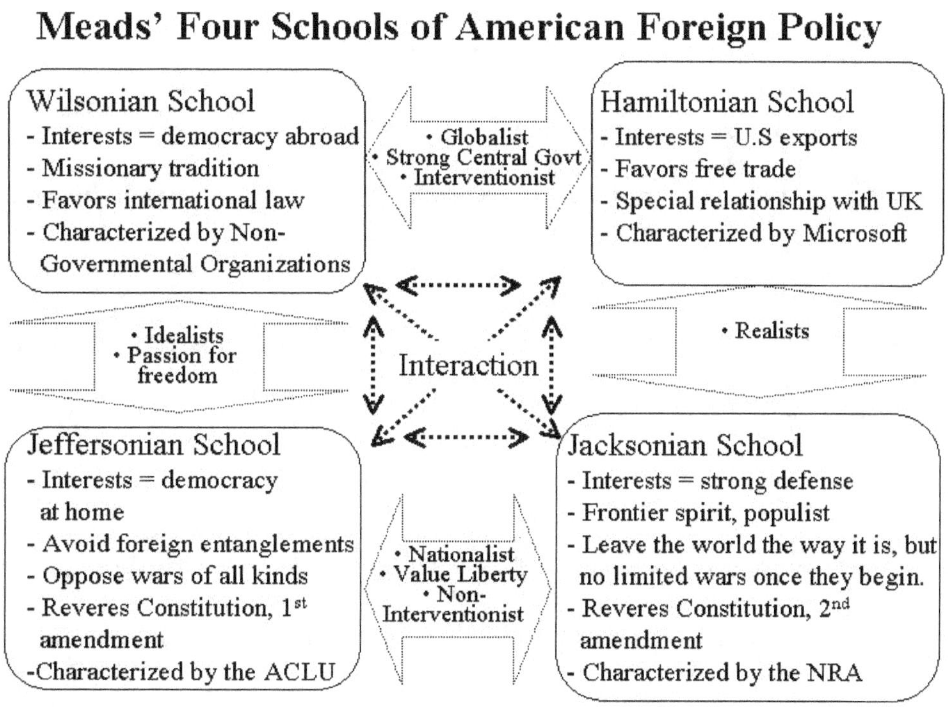

Meads' Four Schools of American Foreign Policy

Wilsonian School
- Interests = democracy abroad
- Missionary tradition
- Favors international law
- Characterized by Non-Governmental Organizations

• Globalist
• Strong Central Govt
• Interventionist

Hamiltonian School
- Interests = U.S exports
- Favors free trade
- Special relationship with UK
- Characterized by Microsoft

• Idealists
• Passion for freedom

Interaction

• Realists

Jeffersonian School
- Interests = democracy at home
- Avoid foreign entanglements
- Oppose wars of all kinds
- Reveres Constitution, 1st amendment
-Characterized by the ACLU

• Nationalist
• Value Liberty
• Non-Interventionist

Jacksonian School
- Interests = strong defense
- Frontier spirit, populist
- Leave the world the way it is, but no limited wars once they begin.
- Reveres Constitution, 2nd amendment
- Characterized by the NRA

Figure 1.   Mead's Four Schools of American Foreign Policy

Source: Adapted from Robert Walz's PowerPoint Slide titled "Mead's Thesis of Four Schools of American Security Policy."

Figure 1 attempts to graphically depict the essence of the four schools as well as how they interact. The box in each corner represents the fundamental views of each foreign policy school. The large arrows between pairs of schools show the shared values between those pairs. The small arrows in the center depict how the interactions of all these schools are what bring about American foreign policy.

Relevance of the Four Traditional Foreign Policy Schools

Walter Russell Mead's four traditional foreign policy schools were selected as a framework for analysis since they form a logical basis for comparison of the four *national security strategy reports*. Mead's schools are much more descriptive than labels such as realist/idealist and more faceted than balance of power politics. It is a construct that stands the test of history as well as providing a model for the future. What follows below is a survey of what is being said in the fields of foreign policy and history about *Special Providence*.

David M. Kennedy, a Pulitzer Prize winning history professor at Stanford University states, "Mead makes a heroic effort to comprehend the entirety of Americans' diplomatic past in a complex structure composed of four "schools" of foreign policy. The interplay among those schools, he claims, is what makes American foreign policy both distinctive and successful . . . . Special Providence remains a rich and substantial book that is sure to influence discussion of foreign-policy issues in the years ahead" (Kennedy 2002, 36).

Even critics, like James P. Rubin, a former Assistant Secretary of State says that:

Mead's framework for the analysis of foreign policy strikes me as at least conceptually adequate. The schools that he portrays do represent the competing currents that a policy-maker in Washington faces today. His framework is certainly more precise than the old categories of hawk and dove, left and right, internationalist and isolationist, unilateralist and multilateralist. (Rubin 2002, 30)

Another critic, Professor C. Dale Walton of South West Missouri State University stated that "no theoretical model can fully account for historical reality in all its depth and nuance" still, "Mead does a fine job of illustrating the diverse intellectual influences that have shaped American foreign policy over the years" (Walton 2002, 425).

Arnold Beichman wrote in *The National Review*, that he chiefly agrees with Mead, and states, "His conclusion is that the competition to influence our foreign policy has had a beneficial effect, much like that of Adam Smith's famous 'invisible hand': 'The endless, unplanned struggle among the schools and lobbies to shape American foreign policy ended up producing over the long run a foreign policy that more closely approximated the true needs and interests of American society than could any conscious design.' This is a valuable insight" (2002, 57).

Additionally, the internationally distinguished *Economist* magazine declared *Special Providence* "one of the finest books of 2001" (2001, 9). Also, the book is frequently part of the core curriculm at many prestigious postgraduate programs, like Johns Hopkins University School of Advanced International Studies (Johns Hokins University 2003), and the National War College (National War College 2003).

Mead's four foreign policy schools are quoted by other famous scholars of all persuasions when writing on foreign affairs. A notable example is Joseph S. Nye, Dean of the Kennedy School of Government at Harvard University, who used Mead's framework in his recent Foreign Affairs article titled *U.S. Power and Strategy After Iraq* (Nye 2003a, 64).

A final reason for Mead's model to function as a good framework for this research is that his four traditional schools also speak to the future of American foreign policy. As H.W. Brands wrote in *National Interest,* "Mead's own evidence strongly suggests that all four schools will be always with us--regardless of what pundits and American diplomats might desire--for they reflect profound aspects of the American character" (Brands 2001, 146).

CHAPTER 3.

THE NATIONAL SECURITY STRATEGY REPORT

The Requirement and Purpose for the *National Security Strategy Report*

The post-World War II organizations and concepts for US national security are derived from the National Security Act of 1947. The purpose of the law created the DOD, the National Security Council (NSC), the Central Intelligence Agency, and was to "provide a comprehensive program for the future security of the United States; to provide for the establishment of integrated policies and procedures for the departments, agencies, and functions of the Government relating to the national security" (United States Congress, 1947). The Act also specifies that the National Security Council will have a critical integration role.

"The function of the Council shall be to advise the President with respect to the integration of domestic, foreign, and military policies relating to the national security so as to enable the military services and the other departments and agencies of the Government to cooperate more effectively in matters involving the national security." (United States Congress 1947, section 402).

Congress has modified this act numerous times, and most significantly in 1986 with the Goldwater-Nichols Department of Defense Reorganization Act. One of the many changes this act included was a requirement for the President to submit an annual NSSR to Congress. It was intended to be an all-encompassing document that explained US national interests, mid-range and long-term strategic goals, and the use of the instruments of national power.

Section 603 of the 1986 Goldwater-Nichols Act specifies the requirements for the

NSSR

(a)(1) The President shall transmit to Congress each year a comprehensive report on the national security strategy of the United States (hereinafter in this section referred to as a 'national security strategy report').

(2) The national security strategy report for any year shall be transmitted on the date on which the President submits to Congress the budget for the next fiscal year under section 1105 of title 31, United States Code.

(b) Each national security strategy report shall set forth the national security strategy of the United States and shall include a comprehensive description and discussion of the following:

(1) The worldwide interests, goals, and objectives of the United States that are vital to the national security of the United States.

(2) The foreign policy, worldwide commitments, and national defense capabilities of the United States necessary to deter aggression and to implement the national security strategy of the United States.

(3) The proposed short-term and long-term uses of the political, economic, military, and other elements of the national power of the United States to protect or promote the interests and achieve the goals and objectives referred to in paragraph (1).

(4) The adequacy of the capabilities of the United States to carry out the national security strategy of the United States, including an evaluation of the balance among the capabilities of all elements of the national power of the United States to support the implementation of the national security strategy.

(5) Such other information as may be necessary to help inform Congress on matters relating to the national security strategy of the United States.

(c) Each national security strategy report shall be transmitted in both a classified and an unclassified form. (United States Congress, 1986, section 603)

Now that the requirement for the NSSR has been established, the thesis will turn to the topic of the international security environment that each of the four selected NSSRs were created to address.

<u>Selected Strategic Environments and Respective *National Security Strategy Reports*</u>

As stated in chapter 2, the thesis will now set the stage for each report by noting the international security environment of the time for each strategy before describing the four selected *national security strategy report*s themselves. The *Strategic Survey,* from the International Institute for Strategic Studies (IISS) will provide consistency when describing the international security environment as well as the prevailing strategic concepts of the time. Once this thesis introduces an overview of the international security environment, the thesis will then describe the composition of the NSSRs from 1988, 1991, 1996, and 2001.

<u>Strategic Environment and the 1988 National Security Strategy of the United States</u>

The late 1980s saw the end of the cold war drawing near. In 1987 and 1988 started to see another warming of relations between the United States and the Soviet Union. The January 1988 *National Security Strategy Report* immediately followed the historic December 1987 summit meeting between Ronald Reagan and Mikhail Gorbachev in Washington (International Institute for Strategic Studies 1988, 5).

In fact, the *Strategic Survey: 1987-1988* foresaw the collapse of the bi-polar world

> It has been clear for some time that the international economic and security order that developed at the end of World War II no longer reflected new realities. A bipolar world developing into a multipolar one; what was once considered a monolithic Communist threat had shattered into many pieces; the over-whelming economic strength of the US in relation to other economic units in East Asia and Western Europe had been declining; and security doctrines worked out for a period of Western nuclear superiority were creating doubts in a time of nuclear parity. The Soviet Union's status of co-equality with the American super-power, established predominantly on the basis of military strength, is threatened in the long run by prolonged and profound economic and social decline – a situation which has prompted an avowed policy of focusing on domestic reconstruction. If recent Soviet rhetoric is fully backed by significant actions to diminish tension

and enhance stability and security (including the shelving of policies aimed at European-US defense coupling) an opportunity – indeed a requirement – for new thinking by the US and its allies will have arisen. (International Institute for Strategic Studies 1988, 5-6)

The 1988 *National Security Strategy of the United States* from President Ronald Regan was still a Soviet focused strategy that centered on countering the Communist aggression and strategic nuclear deterrence. The preface of this strategy succinctly describes his major goals:

> In last years report noted that, at the outset of this Administration, had set forth four broad objectives that underpinned our National Security Strategy. They were:
>
> First, to restore our nation's military strength after a period of decline in which the Soviet Union overtook us in many critical categories of military power;
>
> Second, to restore our nation's economic strength and reinvigorate the world economic system;
>
> Third, to restore the nation's international prestige as a world leader; and
>
> Fourth, to restore pride among all Americans and carry our message to the world that individuals and not governments should control their economic, spiritual and political destinies.
>
> Our National Security Strategy continues to be aimed at reinforcing the gains we have achieved in each of these areas, while employing all the elements of our national power-political, economic and military-in a coordinated way to advance the full range of national security interests outlined elsewhere in this report. (Reagan 1988, iv)

President Reagan cautiously acknowledged the positive developments coming from the Soviet Union stating, "We will welcome real changes, but we have yet to see any slackening of the growth of Soviet military power, or abandonment of expansionist aspirations." (Reagan 1988, v). The rest of the NSSR explains his strategy to counter the Soviet threats worldwide and identified "the most significant threat to U.S. national interests remains that posed by the Soviet Union" (Reagan 1988, 26).

The NSSR goes on to specifically address the policy for the use of the diplomatic, military, informational, and economic instruments of national power as well as addressing strategies for every region in the world. The plan for the integration of these instruments and the regional strategies reflect a policy of containing the Soviet Union and resisting their efforts around the world (Reagan 1988, 7).

Strategic Environment and the 1991 National Security Strategy of the United States

The period of 1989 to 1991 saw some radical changes in the international security environment. The Berlin wall was torn down, the Soviet Union was undergoing a democratic revolution, Iraq invaded Kuwait, and long repressed ethnic tensions were surfacing violently. The early 1990s saw the other rising issues such as the environment and the World Wide Web released.

President George H. W. Bush first spoke of the now famous "new world order" in 1990 saying states should "advance the cause of peace and the fraternity among all nations, to stand for eradication of injustice and the elimination of war and violence, and to contribute to the construction of a new world order--a world in which all nations, big or small, have a right to live in peace and dignity" (Bush 1990).

The *Strategic Survey: 1990-1991* concisely describes this end of the Cold War period below

> The invasion of Kuwait by Iraq and the resulting Gulf war were a rude shock to a world that had expected the end of the Cold War to mean the beginning of an era of peace . . . For as pleasant as it would be to find that the successful conclusion of the war allowed an easy transition to a New World Order, it is more likely that obstinate international problems will continue to create obstacles that will frustrate the most firmly-held intentions and best laid plans for such an order.
>
> A number of other illusions were punctured during the course of 1990. While it was realistic to cheer the removal of communist control from most of the states of eastern Europe, it was not realistic to expect that this would mean a smooth passage to political freedom and economic prosperity in all those nations.

22

Indeed, clearing up the detritus left by the authoritarian regimes has been revealed as a more difficult task than any but the most pessimistic had imagined. Not only have the economies proved more backward than expected, but when the heavy rock of communist repression was lifted a number of nasty nationalist and ethnic issues crawled out. This is particularly true in the southern tier of eastern European states, but even Czechoslovakia's unity could be sundered by Slovakian demands for sovereignty.

The new freedom to express nationalist desires also swept through the Soviet Union. This has had a devastating impact on the Soviet leadership, and threatens to turn it back to the practices of the past, which have little chance of succeeding against the backdrop of economic collapse . . . While the Soviet Union can play a serious spoiling role in the search for a new order in the world, it can no longer provide an alternative vision . . . The USSR retains the military capability of a major power, but its fracturing political edifice and the weakness of its economic foundations belie any pretensions to global leadership. (International Institute for Strategic Studies 1991, 5-6)

In 1991 Iraqi forces were pushed out of Kuwait by the coalition and a cease-fire was in effect by April 1991. In August 1991 the National Security Strategy of the United States was submitted to Congress. This new strategy reflected the administration's views that the Cold War had ended and a new and uncertain but hopeful period was upon them. However, there was still acknowledgment that the Soviet Union posed a threat since it was "the only state possessing the physical military capability to destroy American society with a single, cataclysmic attack" (Bush 1991, iv).

The NSSR of 1991 addressed this new period by stating; "Shaping a security strategy for a new era will require an understanding of the extraordinary trends at work today--a clear picture of what has changed and what has not, an accurate sense of the opportunities that history has put before us and a sober appreciation of the dangers that remain (Bush 1991, 1).

The Strategy goes on to identify regional trends around the world and highlight significant factors such as the importance of North Atlantic Treaty Organization (NATO) to European stability (Bush 1991, 7). This portion of the strategy does not delineate specific regional policies, however it illuminates issues such as; "The powerful

centrifugal forces in Yugoslavia are particularly worrisome" (Bush 1991, 8).

In the 1991 NSSR President Bush specified nine "principles" to guide his national

security strategy

> 1) reinforcing the moral ties that hold our alliances together, even as perceptions of a common security threat change;
>
> 2) encouraging the constructive evolution of the Soviet Union, recognizing the limits of our influence and the continuing power of Soviet military forces;
>
> 3) supporting the independence and vitality of the new Eastern European democracies even as we deal with the uncertainties of the Soviet future;
>
> 4) championing the principles of political and economic freedom as the surest guarantors of human progress and happiness, as well as global peace;
>
> 5) working with others in the global community to resolve regional disputes and stem the proliferation of advanced weapons;
>
> 6) cooperating with the Soviet Union and others in achieving arms control agreements that promote security and stability;
>
> 7) reducing our defense burden as appropriate, while restructuring our forces for new challenges;
>
> 8) tending more carefully to our own economic competitiveness as the foundation of our long-term strength; and
>
> 9) addressing the new global agenda of refugee flows, drug abuse and environmental degradation. (Bush 1991, 34-35)

Strategic Environment and the 1996 A National Security Strategy
 of Engagement and Enlargement

The mid-1990s was a tumultuous one both domestically and in the international

realm. Governor Clinton campaigned for President on a platform focusing on the

domestic economy, but inherited some overseas problems, such as Bosnia and Somalia.

In Somalia he withdrew US forces that were originally deployed for humanitarian reasons

after a failed raid in 1993. In 1995 President Clinton brought a peace agreement to fruition between the warring factions in Bosnia and backed it up by deploying thousands of American soldiers along with other nations to enforce the agreement. The *Strategic Survey* for this period describes the times below

> For Western countries, the present absence of a formal external threat reinforces their introverted tendencies. Notwithstanding the unsettled nature of the contemporary world, a feeling of security permeates the major industrialized nations. The conflicts that rage in many parts of the developing world are localized, internal conflagrations — and while a humanitarian impulse can sometimes move states to intervene, this rarely lasts long enough to create support for lengthy foreign entanglements. The Cold War tendency to see core interests indirectly at stake in distant parts of the globe has now totally eroded. Even the brief post-Cold War sense of 'humanitarian obligation' has begun to give way to colder *realpolitik* calculations of what can be done . . .

> The United States Leads the Way

> The beginning of the 1995 Congressional session set the scene for a political stand-off in the United States. Not only had the electorate returned a Republican majority, but that majority had a radical domestic program that reduced the President's role in domestic legislation to that of an opposition voice armed with a veto. President Clinton turned instead to foreign policy as an arena in which he could make a positive impact. Yet, even in this sphere, he found it necessary to placate both his Republican adversaries in Congress and the conservative-minded US electorate. The struggle for domestic position and electoral favor, particularly in an election year, impinged heavily on the creation and implementation of US foreign policy (International Institute for Strategic Studies 1997, 5-6).

President Clinton released the NSSR in February 1996. This NSSR emphasized the varied security environment of times. President Clinton addressed these threats in his preface

> The dangers we face today are more diverse. Ethnic conflict is spreading and rogue states pose a serious danger to regional stability in many corners of the globe. The proliferation of weapons of mass destruction represents a major challenge to our security. Large-scale environmental degradation, exacerbated by rapid population growth, threatens to undermine political stability in many countries and regions. And the threat to our open and free society from the organized forces of terrorism, international crime and drug trafficking is greater as the technological revolution, which holds such promise, also empowers these destructive forces with novel means to challenge our security. These threats to our security have no respect for boundaries and it is clear that American security in

the 21st Century will be determined by the success of our response to forces that operate within as well as beyond our borders. (Clinton 1996, 1)

The title of this NSSR is *A National Security Strategy of Engagement and Enlargement* which the core premise is "ensuring America remains engaged in the world and by enlarging the community of secure, free market and democratic nations" (Clinton 1996, 2). This theme served as a constant throughout the entire strategy. The NSSR then describes what it calls the three central components of the strategy

(1) our efforts to enhance our security by maintaining a strong defense capability and employing effective diplomacy to promote cooperative security measures;

(2) our work to open foreign markets and spur global economic growth; and

(3) our promotion of democracy abroad.

The NSSR of 1996 also addresses "integrated regional approaches" which "highlights the application of our strategy to each of the world's regions; our broad objectives and thrust, rather than an exhaustive list of all our policies and interests." (Clinton 1996, 42). These regional strategies dealt with the focus for Europe and Eurasia, East Asia and the Pacific, the Western Hemisphere, the Middle East and West Asia, and finally Africa (Clinton 1996, 43-52).

This NSSR then does something unique by describing criteria for commitment of US forces as a reflection of American interests. This is interesting because this NSSR had not clearly identified US interests, but discussed "central goals", "objectives", and "components" of strategy. This NSSR introduced the hierarchy of national interests as vital, important, and humanitarian as well as recent examples

There are three basic categories of national interests that can merit the use of our armed forces. The first involves America's vital interests, that is, interests that are of broad, overriding importance to the survival, security and vitality of our national entity--the defense of U.S. territory, citizens, allies and our economic well-being. We will do whatever it takes to defend these interests, including--when necessary--the unilateral and decisive use of military power. This was demonstrated clearly in the Persian Gulf through Desert Storm and, more recently, Vigilant Warrior, when Iraq threatened aggression against Kuwait in October 1994.

The second category includes cases in which important, but not vital, U.S. interests are threatened. That is, the interests at stake do not affect our national survival, but they do affect importantly our national well-being and the character of the world in which we live. In such cases, military forces should only be used if they advance U.S. interests, they are likely to be able to accomplish their objectives, the costs and risks of their employment are commensurate with the interests at stake and other means have been tried and have failed to achieve our objectives. Such uses of force should also be selective and limited, reflecting the relative saliency of the interests we have at stake. Haiti and Bosnia are the most recent examples in this category.

The third category involves primarily humanitarian interests. Here, our decisions focus on the resources we can bring to bear by using unique capabilities of our military rather than on the combat power of military force. Generally, the military is not the best tool to address humanitarian concerns. But under certain conditions, the use of our armed forces may be appropriate: when a humanitarian catastrophe dwarfs the ability of civilian relief agencies to respond . . . and when the risk to American troops is minimal. The relief operation in Rwanda is a good case in point . . .

The decision on whether and when to use force is therefore dictated first and foremost by our national interests. In those specific areas where our vital or survival interests are at stake, our use of force will be decisive and, if necessary, unilateral. (Clinton 1996, 23)

Strategic Environment and the 2002 The National Security Strategy
 of the United States of America

The world changed for many on 11 September 2001, and this radically altered the

diplomatic policy, defense policy, and foreign aid priorities of the US government. Just

when many thought the world had settled into the post-Cold War period, much of it

changed. The *Strategic Survey: 2001-2002* addressed the period below:

For most of 2001, world affairs stumbled along, as they had for most of the post-Cold War nineties. The consuming issues were Iraq; the Middle East; missile defense and European worries about American unilateralism; proliferation of weapons of mass-destruction (WMD); free trade and globalization; AIDS in Africa; and peacekeeping worries in the face of persistent insurgencies and fraught peace processes across the globe. On 11 September 2001, terrorists in Osama bin Laden's al-Qaeda network steered two hijacked passenger airliners into the World Trade Center in New York and another into the Pentagon outside of Washington DC, and crashed a fourth--probably bound for the White House--in western Pennsylvania. Over 3,000 people representing over 40 nationalities--most of them Americans and virtually all of them civilians--were killed. By signaling the mass-casualty intent and capabilities of transnational Islamic terrorists, and their resistance to deterrence or political suasion, the event transformed international affairs. While international security was cast into disarray, international relations acquired a new, if grimly realist, clarity. America had been shown to be vulnerable at home. US security was at stake. If the US were not able to respond in an effective manner to the act of war perpetrated on its own territory, the US and its friends would become fair game. To reaffirm US global leadership, Washington would need to move towards extroversion and engagement . . . Containing and ultimately defeating terrorism is a formidable task, offering as much scope for disagreement as for cooperation. Yesterday's sense of emotional solidarity is today's shared political burden. It needs to be handled with economic finesse, political savvy, military firmness and moral resolve in careful balance. In the early stages of the containment effort bilateral relationships between the United States and allies, friends, tentative coalition partners and old adversaries will be most important. In this sense, 11 September has re-affirmed that the state remains the basic and indispensable constituent of the international system. (International Institute for Strategic Studies 2002, 5,14)

When the 2002 NSSR was released one year after the world trade center attacks, a "war on terror" had been declared and the Taliban and al-Qaeda had been tactically defeated in Afghanistan by a coalition led by the United States. The strategy redefines threats to the United States by stating, "America is now threatened less by conquering states than we are by failing ones. We are menaced less by fleets and armies than by catastrophic technologies in the hands of the embittered few" (Bush 2002, 1).

President George W. Bush declared in the introduction to the 2002 NSSR that

we seek to create a balance of power that favors human freedom: conditions in which all nations and all societies can choose for themselves the rewards and challenges of political and economic liberty. In a world that is safe, people will be able to make their own lives better. We will defend the peace by fighting terrorists and tyrants. We will preserve the peace by building good relations among the great powers. We will extend the peace by encouraging free and open societies on every continent. (Bush 2002, i)

This new strategy reflected the realities of the post 11 September world. Nations who had been considered a challenge, such as China, were now embraced. The NSSR states, "Today, the world's great powers find ourselves on the same side--united by common dangers of terrorist violence and chaos" (Bush 2002, ii). Another change for President Bush was the new importance on bringing the rest of the world along by saying, "We will actively work to bring the hope of democracy, development, free markets, and free trade to every corner of the world" (Bush 2002, ii). The most controversial component of this NSSR was the explicit threat of pre-emptive attack on terrorists and holders of weapons of mass destruction where "as a matter of common sense and self-defense, America will act against such emerging threats before they are fully formed" (Bush 2002, ii).

CHAPTER 4.

ANALYSIS OF THE NATIONAL SECURITY STRATEGY REPORTS

Analyzing the Requirements of the Goldwater-Nichols Act

This section of the research will address how each of the selected *national security strategy report*s measured up to the two statutory requirements of the Goldwater-Nichols Defense Reorganization Act. As addressed above, this thesis will look at how well each NSSR deals with the following two items from the Act

> (1) The worldwide interests, goals, and objectives of the United States that are vital to the national security of the United States.

> (3) The proposed short-term and long-term uses of the political, economic, military, and other elements of the national power of the United States to protect or promote the interests and achieve the goals and objectives referred to in paragraph (1). (United States Congress, 1986)

National Power Revisited

The elements or instruments of national power were defined in chapter one as diplomatic, informational, military, and economic. However, the Goldwater-Nichols Act specifically mentions only diplomatic, military, and economic. There are a myriad of potential reasons why Congress said, "the other" instruments of national power instead of being more specific. Research into the instruments of national power consistently reveals the existence of at least four instruments; however, only the three instruments of diplomatic, military, and economic are constant.

What then of the fourth instrument of national power? Carnes Lord; who served on the National Security Council staff for President Reagan, emphasizes that the fourth instrument of national power is "strategic intelligence" and goes on to mention domestic political factors (Lord 1988, 91). James C. Gaston writes in *Grand Strategy and the*

Decisionmaking Process that the other instruments of power are "psychological" and "technological" (1992, 72). An even broader definition of power in relation to national security is "Power is multilevel and combined political, psychological, moral, informational, economic, societal, military, police, and civil bureaucratic activity that can be brought to bear" (Manwaring et al. 2003, 37).

There is no clear academic consensus on what the fourth instrument of power is. In chapter 1, this research identified that the instruments of national power rarely fall within the authority of a sole government agency. In fact, these government agencies can work at cross-purposes. "National policies in these various fields are often overlapping, and may even be contradictory. There are seldom "purely military" or "purely political" objectives" (Lykke 1989, 5).

The problem of conflicting intentions is especially true of the informational instrument of power where no one agency is in charge and divergent messages come from multiple departments. Given these circumstances, and the fact that Congress did not specify what the "other instruments" of national power are, this research will only address the diplomatic, military, and economic aspects of the NSSRs.

Three Grand Strategy Questions: Ends, Ways, and Means Revisited

The term "national interest" is an excellent term to describe the fundamental nature and values of a country, but has virtually no meaning in a strategy or national policy. It is in the US interest to have every person in the world healthy, educated, employed, represented in government, and drinking a Coke, but this is valueless for a strategy. This research will strive for a more clear-cut evaluation of national security strategies than what Congress called for in asking for the hazy terms "interests, objectives and goals".

This thesis will instead look for "ends, ways, and means" as defined in chapter 1 to answer this requirement from Goldwater-Nichols. Additionally, a NSSR is an overarching strategy and will not normally address specific subordinate strategies or details such as programs (means). This research will therefore look to answer the following three grand strategy questions for each NSSR:

> 1) What is important to this President in regards to national security? (values, interests, aspirations)
>
> 2) What does this President want to achieve with national security? (ends, objectives, goals)
>
> 3) How does this President intend on reaching those ends? (ways, uses of national power, and occasional means)

Now this thesis will look at how well each NSSR met the requirements of Goldwater-Nichols to identify national security interests and objectives as well as the use of the instruments of national power using these three questions as the vehicle.

The 1988 NSSR Compared to Goldwater-Nichols

The 1988 *National Security Strategy Report* did identify what President Reagan viewed as important, answering our first grand strategy question. The NSSR addressed the administration's view of what was important to the president by first listing the five US interests as

> 1. The survival of the United States as a free and independent nation, with its fundamental values intact and its institutions and people secure.
>
> 2. A healthy and growing U.S. economy to provide opportunity for individual prosperity and a resource base for our national endeavors.
>
> 3. A stable and secure world, free of major threats to U.S. interests.

4. The growth of human freedom, democratic institutions, and free market economies throughout the world, linked by a fair and open international trading system.

5. Healthy and vigorous alliance relationships (Reagan 1988, 3).

Next the 1988 *National Security Strategy Report* described US national security objectives as "broad goals refined from our national interests. They provide a general guide for strategy in specific situations which call for the coordinated use of national power" (Reagan 1988, 26). This answers the second grand strategy question this research addresses by identifying what the president wants to achieve with the below five major objectives or ends:

1. To maintain the security of our nation and our allies. The United States, in cooperation with its allies, must seek to deter any aggression that could threaten that security and, should deterrence fail, must be prepared to repel or defeat any military attack and end the conflict on terms favorable to the United States, its interests, and its allies.

2. To respond to the challenges of the global economy. Our national security and economic strength are indivisible. As the global economy evolves in increasingly interdependent ways, we must be aware of economic factors that may affect our national security, now or in the future. Since our dependence on foreign sources of supply has grown in many critical areas, the potential vulnerability of our supply lines is a matter of concern. Additionally, the threat of a global spiral of protectionism must be combatted, and the problem of debt in the developing world is a burden on international prosperity.

3. To defend and advance the cause of democracy, freedom, and human rights throughout the world. To ignore the fate of millions around the world who seek freedom betrays our national heritage and over time would endanger our own freedom and that of our allies.

4. To resolve peacefully disputes which affect U.S. interests in troubled regions of the world. Regional conflicts which involve allies or friends of the United States may threaten U.S. interests, and frequently pose the risk of escalation to wider conflagration. Conflicts or attempts to subvert friendly governments, which are instigated or supported by the Soviets and their client states, represent a particularly serious threat to the international system and thereby to U.S. interests,

5. To build effective and friendly relationships with all nations whom there is a basis of shared concern. In the world today, there are over 150 nations. Not one of them is the equal of the United States in total power or wealth, but each is sovereign, and most, if not all, touch U.S. interests directly or indirectly. (Reagan 1988, 3-4)

The 1988 *National Security Strategy Report* does address how the government is going to strive to attain these ends by outlining a vision for subordinate policies. The strategy answers the third grand strategy question of this thesis by identifying overarching policies for defense, diplomacy, and international economics as well as supporting space and intelligence policies. For a diplomatic policy, the NSSR addresses "Working with our allies and friends, we have sought to push beyond the stalemates of the postwar era and directly confront two transcendent issues affecting our national security—the danger of nuclear war are and the continuing expansion of totalitarian rule . . . and the ultimate objectives of U.S. foreign policy: peace, yes, but world freedom as well" (Reagan 1988, 9-10).

When outlining the international economic policy, the 1988 NSSR specified the following economic concepts

> Market economies are interdependent. Since 1945, we have pursued a vigorous policy, first, of helping rebuild the European and Pacific economies devastated by war; and second, of supporting economic cooperation and development among all Free World economies. We strongly believed then—as we do now—that national economic strength is a shared strength . . . Internationally, we have led in the coordination of economic policy among the major industrialized countries. In addition, we will continue to assist developing countries to realize sustained, non-inflationary growth, since we understand that this is in our mutual economic and security interest. (Reagan 1988, 11-12)

For defense policy, the 1988 *National Security Strategy Report* went into significant detail in nine pages describing the defense priorities and emphasis. The focused of the policy includes strategic and conventional deterrence, arms control, and maintaining a national mobilization base. Directly girding the defense policies are the two supporting strategies for space and intelligence (Reagan 1988, 13-23).

The 1991 NSSR Compared to Goldwater-Nichols

President George H. W. Bush clearly identifies what is important for national security with his 1991 strategy, answering our first grand strategy question. The 1991 NSSR lists the US national security interests and objectives in the 1990s. Without clearly differentiating between interests and objectives, the 1991 NSSR describes the following four interests

> 1) Survival of the United States as a free and independent nations with its fundamental values intact and its institutions and people secure . . .
>
> 2) A healthy and growing U.S. economy to ensure opportunity for individual prosperity and resources for national endeavors at home and abroad . . .
>
> 3) Healthy, cooperative and politically vigorous relations with allies and friendly nations . . .
>
> 4) A stable and secure world, where political and economic freedom, human rights and democratic institutions flourish (Bush 1991, 3-5).

The 1991 NSSR answers our second grand strategy question by identifying the ends the President wanted to accomplish in national security with objectives. Under the interest of survival of the United States, President Bush listed eight objectives.

> -- deter any aggression . . . repel or defeat military attack . . .
>
> -- effectively counter threats . . . including the threat of international terrorism;
>
> -- . . . verifiable arms control agreements . . . defending against limited ballistic-missile strikes, and enhancing . . . conventional capabilities;
>
> -- promote democratic change in the Soviet Union . . .
>
> -- foster restraint in global military spending and discourage military adventurism;
>
> -- prevent the transfer . . . to hostile countries or groups . . . of chemical, biological and nuclear weapons and . . . high-technology means of delivery;

35

-- reduce the flow of illegal drugs. (Bush 1991, 3-4)

Under the national interest of a healthy and growing economy, President Bush pursued four objectives, or ends, for national security. These include

-- promote a strong, prosperous and competitive U.S. economy;

-- ensure access to foreign markets, energy, mineral resources, the oceans and space;

-- promote an open and expanding international economic system, based on market principles, with minimal distortions to trade and investment, stable currencies . . . .

-- achieve cooperative international solutions to key environmental challenges, assuring the sustainability and environmental security of the planet as well as growth and opportunity for all. (Bush 1991, 4)

The 1991 NSSR specifies five objectives for the interest of friendly relations with allies and friends. Theses five objectives are

-- strengthen and enlarge the commonwealth of free nations that share a commitment to democracy and individual rights;

-- establish a more balanced partnership with our allies and a greater sharing of global leadership and responsibilities;

-- strengthen international institutions like the United Nations to make them more effective in promoting peace, world order and political, economic and social progress;

-- support Western Europe's historic march toward greater economic and political unity . . .

-- work with our North Atlantic allies to . . . bring about reconciliation, security and democracy in a Europe whole and free. (Bush 1991, 4-5)

Finally, the president identified five more objectives related to the interest of a stable and secure world "where political and economic freedom, human rights and democratic institutions flourish" (Bush 1991, 5). These five objectives are

-- maintain stable regional military balances to deter those powers that might seek regional dominance;

-- promote diplomatic solutions to regional disputes;

-- promote the growth of free, democratic political institutions as the surest guarantors of both human rights and economic and social progress;

-- aid in combatting threats to democratic institutions from aggression, coercion, insurgencies, subversion, terrorism and illicit drug trafficking;

-- support aid, trade and investment policies that promote economic development and social and political progress.

The 1991 NSSR then identifies the use of the instruments of national power, thus answering our third grand strategy question of how the President plans to achieve these objectives. The strategy outlines specific focus for diplomatic, economic, and military policies to support the strategy. Under diplomacy there is a new emphasis on the importance of the United Nations in solving issues as it had supported the coalition in ousting Iraq from Kuwait (Bush 1991, 13). The diplomatic section also emphasized nurturing democracy abroad, arms control, stemming the proliferation of weapons of mass destruction (WMD), foreign aid programs, illicit drug trafficking, and immigration (Bush 1991, 14-19).

The economic focus emphasized a strong domestic economy and "a strategy that expands and strengthens market economies around the world." (Bush 1991, 20). This economic strategy contained the elements of reducing the US trade deficit, debt reduction for developing nations, expanding free trade, and controlling the proliferation of dangerous technologies (Bush 1991, 20-22). The NSSR also addressed secure energy supplies, environmental stewardship, and the importance of the freedom to explore and utilize outer space (Bush 1991, 23-25).

Despite just winning the first Gulf War, the NSSR defense agenda included some of the most significant changes for the United States

In a world less driven by an immediate, massive threat to Europe or the danger of global war, the need to support a smaller but still crucial forward presence and to deal with regional contingencies--including possibly a limited, conventional threat to Europe--will shape how we organize, equip, train, deploy and employ our active and reserve forces. We must also have the ability to reconstitute forces, if necessary, to counter any resurgent global threat. (Bush 1991, 25)

The NSSR states that there are four fundamentals for defense policy in this new era

1) to ensure strategic deterrence,
2) to exercise forward presence in key areas,
3) to respond effectively to crises and
4) to retain the national capacity to reconstitute forces should this ever be needed. (Bush 1991, 25)

The military strategy specified in the NSSR of 1991 related the means to ends for defense. The NSSR explained the elements of nuclear deterrence including strategic nuclear forces and limited missile defense. The defense policy stressed the change to limited forward presence while retaining the ability to project forces from the US The NSSR also addressed reducing military strength to a new "base force" that planned for downsizing to the minimum force needed for national security. (Bush 1991, 25-28).

The 1996 NSSR Compared to Goldwater-Nichols

President Clinton in the 1996 NSSR identify what the administration views as important in relation to national security by evoking the basic principles contained in the Constitution of the United States. "In a democracy, however, the foreign policy and security strategy of the nation must serve the needs of the people. The preamble of the Constitution sets out the basic objectives: provide for the common defense, promote the general welfare, and secure the blessings of liberty to ourselves and our posterity" (Clinton 1996, 7). This is a much broader and more abstract view of national security.

This 1996 NSSR identified three "central goals" or objectives of US national security, which answers the second grand strategy question of this thesis below:

1) To enhance our security with military forces that are ready to fight and with effective representation abroad.

2) To bolster America's economic revitalization.

3) To promote democracy abroad . . .

These goals are supported by ensuring America remains engaged in the world and by enlarging the community of secure, free market and democratic nations. (Clinton 1996, 2)

The strategy also explains how we are pursuing these goals in specific regions by adapting and constructing institutions that will help to provide security and increase economic growth throughout the world. Specifically, the NSSR rephrases the three goals above into three "central components" that emphasize defense capability, the importance of promoting democracy, and increasing the growth of free trading nations

To that broad end, the three central components of our strategy of engagement and enlargement are: (1) our efforts to enhance our security by maintaining a strong defense capability and employing effective diplomacy to promote cooperative security measures; (2) our work to open foreign markets and spur global economic growth; and (3) our promotion of democracy abroad. (Clinton 1996, 7)

The strategy then addresses five "core principles that guide our policies" (Clinton 1996, 14). These core principles partly answer our third grand strategy question since these principles specify how to attain ends using means:

1) First and foremost, we must exercise global leadership. We are not the world's policeman, but as the word's premier economic and military power, and with the strength of our democratic values, U.S. engagement is indispensable to the forging of stable political relations and open trade to advance our interests.

2) Our leadership must stress preventive diplomacy--through such means as support for democracy, economic assistance, overseas military presence, interaction between U.S. and foreign militaries and involvement in multilateral

negotiations in the Middle East and elsewhere--in order to help resolve problems, reduce tensions and defuse conflicts before they become crises.

3) Our engagement must be selective, focusing on the challenges that are most important our own interests and focusing our resources where we can make the most difference. We must also use the right tools--being willing to act unilaterally when our direct national interests are most at stake . . .

4) In all cases, the nature of our response must depend on what best serves our own long-term national interests . . .

5) Our national security strategy draws upon a range of political, military and economic instruments, and focuses on the primary objectives. (Clinton 1996, 14-15)

The 1996 *National Security Strategy Report* also lists other specific "tasks" for national security that further explain how the administration plans to attain their ends, thus answering the third grand strategy question. For the goal of enhancing security these include providing credible overseas presence, countering weapons of mass destruction proliferation, countering terrorism and drug trafficking, and arms control (Clinton 1996, 17).

The goal of promoting prosperity at home the strategy identifies the policies of international integration, enhancing access to foreign markets, and expanding open markets (Clinton 1996, 34). The 1996 NSSR also mentions the importance of unrestricted access to foreign oil supplies and promoting sustainable development abroad (Clinton 1996, 38).

The goals of promoting democracy is addressed with the statement "All of America's strategic interests--from promoting prosperity at home to checking global threats abroad before they threaten our territory--are served by enlarging the community of democratic and free-market nations. Thus, working with new democratic states to help preserve them as democracies committed to free markets and respect for human rights, is

a key part of our national security strategy" (Clinton 1996, 40).

The essential element in this aspect of ways and means for promoting democracy

is to

> . . . help democracy and free-markets expand and survive in other places where we have the strongest security concerns and where we can make the greatest difference. This is not a democratic crusade; it is a pragmatic commitment to see freedom take hold where that will help us most. Thus, we must target our effort to assist states that affect our strategic interests, such as those with large economies, critical locations, nuclear weapons or the potential to generate refugee flows into our own nation or into key friends and allies. We must focus our efforts where we have the most leverage. And our efforts must be demand-driven--they must focus on nations whose people are pushing for reform or have already secured it. (Clinton 1996, 40)

The 2002 NSSR Compared to Goldwater-Nichols

President George W. Bush identifies what he sees as important with regards to

national security by stating that: "The great strength of this nation must be used to

promote a balance of power that favors freedom. . . . The aim of this strategy is to help

make the world not just safer but better. Our goals on the path to progress are clear:

political and economic freedom, peaceful relations with other states, and respect for

human dignity" (Bush 2002, 1). This statement of intent answers our first grand strategy

question of what does the President view as important for national security.

The 2002 NSSR then lists three broad goals for US national security answering

our second grand strategy question. The goals are 1) political and economic freedom, 2)

peaceful relations with other states, and 3) respect for human dignity (Bush 2002, 1). The

NSSR then immediately addresses our third grand strategy question of ways when it lists

eight areas of emphasis for achieving these goals

1) champion aspirations for human dignity;

41

2) strengthen alliances to defeat global terrorism and work to prevent attacks against us and our friends;

3) work with others to defuse regional conflicts;

4) prevent our enemies from threatening us, our allies, and our friends, with weapons of mass destruction;

5) ignite a new era of global economic growth through free markets and free trade;

6) expand the circle of development by opening societies and building the infrastructure of democracy;

7) develop agendas for cooperative action with other main centers of global power; and

8) transform America's national security institutions to meet the challenges and opportunities of the twenty-first century. (Bush 2002, 1-2)

These eight areas of emphasis that are similar to goals or objectives from other strategies and they serve as a framework for the rest of strategy as each one titles a chapter in the NSSR. Within each chapter addressing each emphasis area, the NSSR identifies specific actions the US government plans to take. This adds detail to the third grand strategy question on how the ends will be attained.

The emphasis area on championing aspirations for human dignity discuss how "America must stand firmly for the nonnegotiable demands of human dignity: the rule of law; limits on the absolute power of the state; free speech; freedom of worship; equal justice; respect for women; religious and ethnic tolerance; and respect for private property" (Bush 2002, 3). The chapter then four specific actions or ways for the US to implement

> --speak out honestly about violations of the nonnegotiable demands of human dignity using our voice and vote in international institutions to advance freedom;
>
> --use our foreign aid to promote freedom and support those who struggle non-violently for it, ensuring that nations moving toward democracy are rewarded . . .

42

--make freedom and the development of democratic institutions key themes in our bilateral relations . . . while we press governments that deny human rights to move toward a better future;

--take special efforts to promote freedom of religion and conscience and defend it from encroachment by repressive governments.

The chapter dealing with strengthening allies to defeat global terrorism and work to prevent attacks is one of the most critical chapters since the terrorist attacks on the US homeland the year before this NSSR. The strategy states "Our priority will be first to disrupt and destroy terrorist organizations of global reach and attack their leadership; command, control, and communications; material support; and finances" (Bush 2002, 5).

The strategy explains the government will help regional partners in the Global War on Terror (GWOT) to "ensure the state has the military, law enforcement, political, and financial tools necessary to finish the task" (Bush 2002, 6). This chapter also addresses the creation of the new Department of Homeland Security, and focuses on state sponsors or terrorists attempting to get or use weapons of mass destruction (WMD) (Bush 2002, 6). To disrupt and destroy terrorist organizations, the strategy identifies three more specific actions:

> -- direct and continuous action using all the elements of national and international power. Our immediate focus will be those terrorist organizations of global reach and any terrorist or state sponsor of terrorism which attempts to gain or use weapons of mass destruction (WMD) or their precursors;

> -- defending the United States, the American people, and our interests at home and abroad by identifying and destroying the threat before it reaches our borders. While the United States will constantly strive to enlist the support of the international community, we will not hesitate to act alone, if necessary, to exercise our right of self-defense by acting preemptively against such terrorists, to prevent them from doing harm against our people and our country; and

> -- denying further sponsorship, support, and sanctuary to terrorists by convincing or compelling states to accept their sovereign responsibilities.

-- We will also wage a war of ideas to win the battle against terrorism . . . to make clear that all acts of terrorism are illegitimate . . . to ensure that the conditions and ideologies that promote terrorism do not find fertile ground in any nation . . . by enlisting the international community to focus its efforts and resources on areas most at risk; and using effective public diplomacy to promote the free flow of information and ideas to kindle the hopes and aspirations of freedom of those in societies ruled by the sponsors of global terrorism. (Bush 2002, 6)

The chapter addressing the emphasis area of defusing regional conflicts by working with others serves the purpose to "avoid explosive escalation and minimize human suffering . . . When violence erupts and states falter, the United States will work with friends and partners to alleviate suffering and restore stability" (Bush 2002, 9).

This area draws from the new outlook the Bush administration took after 11 September 2001 where regional powers had previously been a viewed as competitors which "requires tough realism in our dealings with China and Russia" (Bush 1999, 239). The administration made a significant shift in this strategy and now states,

Today, the world's great powers find ourselves on the same side— united by common dangers of terrorist violence and chaos. The United States will build on these common interests to promote global security. We are also increasingly united by common values. Russia is in the midst of a hopeful transition, reaching for its democratic future and a partner in the war on terror. Chinese leaders are discovering that economic freedom is the only source of national wealth. (Bush 2002, ii)

This area of defusing conflicts has two strategic principles that the administration uses to approach situations. These two principles are "The United States should invest time and resources into building international relationships and institutions that can help manage local crises when they emerge. The United States should be realistic about its ability to help those who are unwilling or unready to help themselves" (Bush 2002, 9).

The section goes on to discuss potential or existing troubled areas and the actions being taken. These include the Israeli-Palestinian conflict, South Asia, and Latin

America. The strategy gets more specific in regards to Africa, and states, "Africa's great size and diversity requires a security strategy that focuses on bilateral engagement and builds coalitions of the willing" (Bush 2002, 11). The NSSR then lists three interlocking strategies to use in Africa such as using the more powerful African states of South Africa, Nigeria, Kenya, and Ethiopia as anchors for regional, coordination with European allies and international institutions, and strengthening reforming states and sub-regional organizations (Bush 2002, 11).

The chapter dealing with the threats from weapons of mass destruction states, "Rogue states and terrorists do not seek to attack us using conventional means. They know such attacks would fail. Instead, they rely on acts of terror and, potentially, the use of weapons of mass destruction--weapons that can be easily concealed, delivered covertly, and used without warning" (Bush 2002, 15). In order to deal with these threats the strategy outlines aggressive policies since "We cannot let our enemies strike first" and "the United States cannot remain idle while dangers gather" the "United States will, if necessary, act preemptively" (Bush 2002, 15).

> We must be prepared to stop rogue states and their terrorist clients before they are able to threaten or use weapons of mass destruction against the United States and our allies and friends. Our response must take full advantage of strengthened alliances, the establishment of new partnerships with former adversaries, innovation in the use of military forces, modern technologies, including the development of an effective missile defense system, and increased emphasis on intelligence collection and analysis. (Bush 2002, 14)

The chapters on free trade and global economic growth and expanding the circle of development are seen by the administration as the "best way to promote prosperity and reduce poverty" (Bush 2002, 17). The focus of these policies are on the rule of law, investment in health and education, free trade, and secure energy for the world (Bush

2002, 17-19). The strategy sets a goal of doubling the world's poorest economies within a decade and increasing US development assistance by fifty percent (Bush 2002, 21). These grants (not loans) will be provided to nations that meet the challenge of reform and set up a new Millennium Challenge Account for justly ruled countries that encourage freedom (Bush 2002, 21-22).

The emphasis area of cooperating with other main centers of global power focus mainly on working with NATO and forming coalitions with Russia, China, and other strong nations to implement this NSSR overall. The next chapter on reforming America's national security institutions state the goals of maintaining military capabilities "beyond challenge" to dissuade any threats and "decisively defeat any adversary if deterrence fails" (Bush 2002, 29). This emphasis area also transforms the US military for the twenty first century, transforms intelligence capabilities, and integrates intelligence with defense, law enforcement, and our allies (Bush 2002, 29).

Analysis with the Four Traditional US Foreign Policy Schools

This segment of the research will evaluate the four selected NSSRs based on what combination of Mead's four traditional foreign policy schools each falls within. This section will only look at what is actually written within each NSSR, and not attempt to evaluate a President based on what is said or done outside the published grand strategy. Again, the four foreign policy schools of thought are Jacksonian, Jeffersonian, Wilsonian, and Hamiltonian. James P. Rubin writing in *New Republic* presented this summary of Mead's thesis:

> We begin with the Hamiltonians. This school is built on the conviction of the
> primacy of international economics. To ensure America's independence and
> prosperity in its early years, the United States had to protect the freedom of the

seas, open the door for our exports around the world, and prevent any other power from challenging these principles . . .

Jefferson's school, according to Mead, was . . . concerned mainly with protecting American democracy against the dangers of executive power and limiting the costs and the risks of whatever foreign policies were necessary to protect our independence. Idealism at home, realism abroad: this was the Jeffersonian motto . . .

The Jeffersonians, beginning with Jefferson, feared that Hamiltonian engagement abroad would lead to a standing army and navy, and new powers for the president, and a weaker congressional oversight role, and a greater degree of secrecy in government. When the Hamiltonians looked around the world, they saw opportunity. The Jeffersonians saw danger. They were the early deficit hawks, believing that wars or conflicts abroad aimed at opening markets would increase the national debt, and benefit mainly the bankers, and oppress the citizenry with higher taxes. Eisenhower's concern about the rise of a military-industrial complex was a supremely Jeffersonian concern . . .

The Wilsonian grand strategy became clear during the extraordinary debate over the League of Nations. It was this modern American school of thought about international affairs that was the first to argue what is accepted wisdom today: that democracies make better, more reliable, and more predictable partners than dictatorships. Like the Jeffersonians, the Wilsonians believed that monarchies and dictators did not reflect the enduring national interests of their countries, but were the egregious causes of needless wars provoked by petty personal quarrels and wild policy swings when governments fell . . .

This notion of democratization as a goal of foreign policy led to the Wilsonians' most important contribution. In seeking to make the world "safe for democracy," they placed the United States on the right side of history as democratic change and independence slowly and fitfully swept across the globe . . .

The Jacksonians . . . arose out of the frontier and the folk culture that Andrew Jackson most perfectly and noisily represented. This view of American foreign policy remains most popular in the Southwest, the Deep South, and parts of the Midwest, where the frontier experience was crucial to the development of local politics. The Jacksonians are the warriors of American society. While they prefer to avoid conflict with the rest of the world and often rail at the complications of economic engagement, they believe that if war comes we should deploy all our power in ruthless pursuit of total victory (Rubin 2002, 29-31).

As discussed in chapter two, "'Hamiltonians' link a strong government with

strong businesses, and they support free trade. 'Wilsonians' emphasize America's democratic mission in the world. 'Jeffersonians' are more protective of American values at home. 'Jacksonians' emphasize military and economic readiness for possible conflict" (Zelikow 2001, 1). This research will determine what mix each NSSR presents.

The 1988 NSSR Analyzed with Mead's Foreign Policy Schools

The main message of the 1988 NSSR is focused on a strong military and alliances to contain and "confront" the Soviet Union by "helping anti-communist insurgents" (Reagan 1988, 7-10). With this in mind there are strong Jacksonian themes that come to the forefront. The combination of the Strategic Defense Initiative (SDI) to defeat Soviet nuclear first strikes in conjunction with arms reductions is clearly Jacksonian (Reagan 1988, 15).

President Reagan's NSSR is not a very Wilsonian document. There are references to Wilsonian principles such as human rights and international institutions, but they take on secondary or supporting importance. For example, the NSSR states "the ultimate objectives of U.S. foreign policy: peace, yes, but world freedom as well. We refuse to believe that it is somehow an act of hostility to proclaim publicly the crucial moral distinctions between democracy and totalitarianism" (Reagan 1988, 10). The strategy lists international organizations and multilateral efforts, but only as an instrument to achieve U.S. objectives (Reagan 1988, 7-8).

There are a number of Hamiltonian themes such as "Market economies are interdependent" and the United States has a responsibility to "extend the global economic recover" (Reagan 1988, 121). However, the Jacksonian comes back out when the strategy states "There are times, however, when we must restrict economic relations between the United States and other countries not only for reasons of national security, but to protest odious national behavior" (Reagan 1988, 12). This research identified no elements that could be considered Jeffersonian.

The 1991 NSSR Analyzed with Mead's Foreign Policy Schools

President George H.W. Bush's 1991 NSSR is clearly a combination Hamiltonian, and to a lesser degree, Wilsonian agenda. The strategy states "America will continue to support an international economic system as open and inclusive as possible, as the best way to strengthen global economic development, political stability and the growth of free societies" (Bush 1991, 2). Hamiltonian concepts are strongly represented in the strategy as the administration pursues eliminating tariffs worldwide and "The United States will continue its efforts to expand trade further" (Bush 1991, 22).

Wilsonian traits come out when the NSSR mentions, "The Gulf crisis interrupted a time of hope. We saw a new world coming, a world freer from the threat of terror, stronger in the pursuit of justice, more secure in the quest for peace. Democracy was gaining ground as were the principles of human rights and political and economic freedom. This new world is still within reach, perhaps brought closer by the unprecedented international cooperation achieved in the Gulf crisis (Bush 1991, 3).

Neither Jacksonian nor Jeffersonian traits are evidenced in this NSSR.

The 1996 NSSR Analyzed with Mead's Foreign Policy Schools

The 1996 NSSR from President Clinton is a strongly Wilsonian strategy with solid Hamiltonian themes. The entire concept of "Engagement and Enlargement" is built on the dual Wilsonian and Hamiltonian pillars.

> Promoting democracy does more than foster our ideals. It advances our interests because we know that the larger the pool of democracies, the better off we, and the entire community of nations, will be. Democracies create free markets that offer economic opportunity, make for more reliable trading partners and are

49

far less likely to wage war on one another. While democracy will not soon take hold everywhere, it is in our interest to do all that we can to enlarge the community of free and open societies. (Clinton 1996, 7)

Neither Jacksonian nor Jeffersonian traits are evidenced in this NSSR. President Clinton advocates a very un-Jacksonian/Jeffersonian policy of using the armed forces whenever our interests are at stake, which include vital, important, and even humanitarian interests.

The 2002 NSSR Analyzed with Mead's Foreign Policy Schools

President George W. Bush presents a very Jacksonian strategy supported by methods that are Wilsonian and Hamiltonian. The entire concept of preemptive attacks and unilateral actions are clearly Jacksonian. The President says in the NSSR "We will actively work to bring the hope of democracy, development, free markets, and free trade to every corner of the world" (Bush 2002, ii). This is a firm merging of Wilsonian and Hamiltonian strategies.

This blending of the three major foreign policy schools has a strong leaning towards Jacksonian since it supports international institutions but do not reign over US sovereignty and therefore "Coalitions of the willing can augment these permanent institutions" (Bush 2002, iii). A close reading of the NSSR chapter five on weapons of mass destruction reveals the administration's opinion that the world to too dangerous to for the United States to be constrained while threatened.

CHAPTER 5.

SYNTHESIS AND CONCLUSIONS

Synthesis

This portion will synthesize, or bring together, the analysis conducted in chapter four. Further, the research will identify what elements of continuity exist between the selected strategies and what elements are dissimilar. The intent is to seek out traits and themes among the four selected NSSRs. Conclusions will follow the synthesis that resulted from the analysis.

Meeting the Requirements of Goldwater-Nichols

Congress was looking for a document explaining the President's vision for national security and how he plans to implement that strategy. In fact the concept of a national security strategy that goes beyond periodic presidential national security directives, decisions, and memorandum came from Packard Commission in the mid-1980s. The Packard Commission recommended a relatively detailed national security strategy to define and prioritize national security objectives, outline major policies, and specify budget planning levels (Packard Commission 1986, 7).

Congress took this concept even farther and wrote even more detailed requirements into the Goldwater-Nichols Department of Defense Reorganization Act. Congress not only wanted to know what the national security objectives were, but how the President planned to use all the instruments of national power and to outline this strategy over time. All of the four NSSRs addressed in this research are lacking in specificity, and are "too vague" (Jordan, Taylor, Korb 1999, 206). The reason for this has to do with primarily with domestic politics. Donald M. Snider, who served in the

National Security Council writing the 1988 NSSR, writes about the tensions between the legislative and executive branches of government and states

> "What President in a fast-paced media-oriented world wants to articulate in a static annual, written report a detailed statement of his forward-looking strategic vision? . . . To influence resource allocations it was considered far better to report mushy 'globaloney' to Congress in written form and to depend instead on current, personal testimonies by Administration officials before the Committees, supported by presidential speeches as part of a coherent and widespread campaign of public diplomacy to the electorate of the United States" (1993, 48).

What each NSSR did do was answer the three more general grand strategy questions asked in this research. Specifically, what does the President view as important to national security, what does he aim to achieve, and how does he plan to accomplish those ends? How then did these different Presidents view US national interests and objectives? A comparison of the paraphrased NSSRs is provided in table one below.

The first observation of this comparison is that neither President Clinton nor President George W. Bush were very specific in their strategy defining national security interests. However, many authors have opined that national interests have remained relatively unchanged since the end of World War II. These interests as addressed in chapter 1 are essentially: (1) preserving US sovereignty, (2) protecting US values, institutions, and people; (3) promoting economic prosperity and (4) a stable world.

Although US administrations may not use the same terms, each of these four interests clearly exist in the four selected NSSRs. This leaves this research with the finding that there are four US national interests of sovereignty, security, stability, and prosperity. The conclusion drawn from this analysis is that these four US national interests are universal regardless of the security environment or the political affiliation of the president.

Table 1. Comparing National Interests and Objectives from Selected NSSRs

	Reagan 1988 NSSR	Bush 1991 NSSR	Clinton 1996 NSSR	Bush 2002 NSSR
Interests	1.Survival of US people, values and institutions. 2. A healthy and growing US economy. 3. A stable and secure world. 4. The growth of human freedom, democracy, and free markets. 5. Healthy and vigorous alliance relationships. (Reagan 1988, 3)	1. Survival of US people, values and institutions. 2. A healthy and growing US economy. 3. Solid relations with allies and friendly nations. 4. A stable and secure world, where political and economic freedom, human rights and democratic institutions flourish. (Bush 1991, 3-5)	*1. provide for the common defense.* *2. promote the general welfare.* *3. secure the blessings of liberty to ourselves and our posterity.* (Clinton 1996,7)	*1. Defend the Nation against its enemies (mainly terrorists) is the first responsibility of Government.* *2. promote a balance of power that favors freedom and make the world not just safer but better, political and economic freedom, peaceful relations with other states.* (Bush 2002, i)
Objectives	1. Deter aggression, repel or defeat attack. 2. Favorable global economy (secure supply lines, reduce protectionism). 3. Advance democracy, freedom, and human rights throughout the world. 4. To resolve disputes peacefully (in favor of US in-terests). 5. To build effective and friendly relationships with all nations. (Reagan 1988, 3-4)	1. Deter aggression, repel or defeat attack. 2. counter threats (terrorism). 3. arms control agreements, defending against ballistic-missiles, and enhancing conventional capabilities. 4. promote democratic change in the Soviet Union. 5. foster restraint in global military spending & adventurism. 6. prevent WMDs and means of delivery getting to hostile groups. 7. reduce the flow of illegal drugs. (Bush 1991, 3-4)	1. To enhance our security with military forces that are ready to fight and with effective representation abroad. 2. To bolster America's economic revitalization. 3 To promote democracy abroad. (Clinton 1996,7)	1. champion aspirations for human dignity 2. defeat global terrorism and work to prevent attacks. 3. work with others to defuse regional conflicts. 4. prevent threats from WMD. 5. ignite global economic growth through free markets and free trade. 6. expand the circle of development and build democracy. 7. cooperative action with other global powers. 8. transform America's natl security for the 21st cent. (Bush 2002, 1-2).

Note: Italicized notes indicated inferred interests and objectives, not specified in NSSR.

However, these interests are too loose a concept to use in specifying a national policy. For example, President Clinton did an excellent job defining a tertiary hierarchy of US interests and described using US military force at each level including vital, important, and humanitarian interests. Where differences can be found between presidents is in their differing national security objectives.

All of these presidents identified objectives that were a product of the security environment each faced. This is why President George H. W. Bush added democratic change in the Soviet Union (and mentioned no other region or state), as well as interdicting illegal drugs. President Clinton focused on enlarging globalization, while President George W. Bush focuses solely on terrorists and their supporters as the threat to the US. How these approaches differ can be codified using Mead's four foreign policy schools.

Mead's Foreign Policy Schools

This section will synthesize how the NSSRs compare to each other in relation to Mead's four foreign policy schools analyzed in chapter 4. As discussed earlier, each President showed characteristics of combining the different schools of US foreign policy as described by Walter Russell Mead. The Jeffersonian school is a perpetual minority, and none of the selected Presidents held any Jeffersonian traits.

A graphic depiction comparing these presidential traits is below in figure 2. This figure depicts the combination of Mead's four foreign policy schools for each president. The placement of an "X" for each president between these schools is supposed to show the weigh of their convictions between one school over the others as determined by the NSSR. If an "X" is closer to the center of a school, that depicts a strong association with that school. If an "X" is near the outer portion of a school represents a secondary conviction for that school. An "X" completely outside a school signifies no subscription to that school in the NSSR.

As shown in chapter 4, President Reagan displayed a Hamiltonian and Jacksonian combination character in the 1988 NSSR. President Reagan is depicted in the figure as an "X" that is clearly within the Hamiltonian school, and someone on periphery of the Jacksonian school, without being in the Wilsonian school. President George H.W. Bush showed a strongly Hamiltonian flavor with Wilsonian elements of favoring international organizations. He is depicted on the figure as in the Hamiltonian school significantly, with one foot in the Wilsonian school. President Clinton is a strong Wilsonian followed closely by Hamiltonian traits. He is depicted on the figure as primarily in the Wilsonian school with overlap into the Hamiltonian school. President George W. Bush is a strong Jacksonian followed by Hamiltonian with some elements of Wilsonian flavor. President George W. Bush is shown as the only president with representation in all three main schools. He is depicted in the figure as equally Jacksonian and Hamiltonian with his "X" being just inside the Wilsonian school.

These traits help depict a President's views on problems and may help predict how the administration will react to certain situations. Since we have determined that US national interests do not change, but these Presidents do have differing objectives, this model may serve as a more useful tool in analyzing Presidential national security policy.

Graphic Depiction of Selected NSSRs
Combination of Mead's Schools

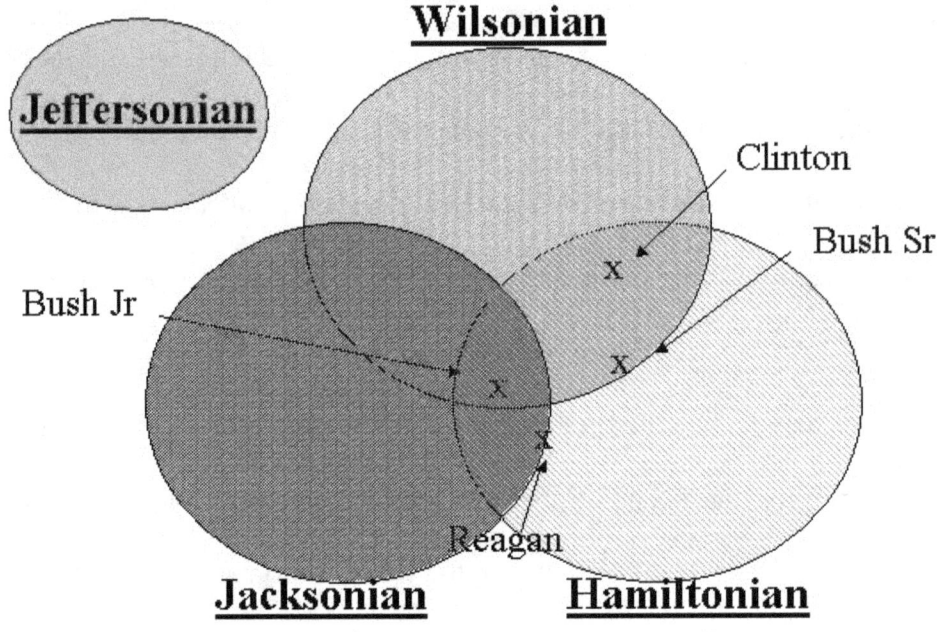

Figure 2.   Charting Selected NSSRs with Mead's Four Schools of Foreign Policy

Conclusions

This research has identified that US interests have remained fundamentally unchanged through all four administrations addressed. However, each administration has uniquely approached the NSSR by identifying different national security objectives and emphasized varied roles for the instruments of national power to achieve these ends. These differing approaches to grand strategy are evidenced by what combination of traits of Mead's four foreign policy schools they possess.

Although these NSSRs do address objectives, there is no specific prioritization among national objectives or guidance to synchronize the multiple government agencies charged to fulfill the strategy. The purpose of the NSSR requirement in Goldwater-Nichols As Don M. Snyder writes, was to address that, "The Executive Branch has more often than not failed to formulate, in an integrated and coherent manner judiciously using resources drawn from all elements of national power, a mid- and long-term strategy necessary to defend and further those interests vital to the nation's security" (Snider and Nagl 2001, 129).

This congressional intent has not been fundamentally met. In fact, an executive agency can write a detailed subordinate strategy (such as a national military strategy) that is in line with the NSSR, but still diverge with another strategy, such as US foreign policy in a certain region or country, even when that other subordinate policy also meets the intent of the NSSR. Take the Clinton administration approach to China for example. Here the military was conducting provocative intelligence gathering flights right up to the Chinese border while US diplomats were negotiating entrance into the World Trade Organization.

In conclusion, these NSSRs do not meet the standards required by the law, and they are too vague to serve as true beacons to guide subordinate policies. Executive agencies should not expect to find truly meaningful direction from the NSSR. This requires the federal government to turn to the NSC and the interagency process to hammer out objectives and policies for a region or nation as required. Instead of a true grand strategy, the United States has placed itself in perpetual crisis action planning mode.

Recommendations for Further Study

There are a number of areas of grand strategy and subordinate policies that lend themselves to further study based on this thesis. For example, a study comparing classified NSSRs would be very useful. These classified reports may very well be more detailed or be more uniform in structure and content. This would better highlight differences and similarities.

Another recommendation for further study is to compare how the NSSRs were implemented. There are a number of different methodologies that would fit such a study, such as studying a specific region, conflict, or threat. For example, a study could examine how the NSSRs were implemented with regard to one or more constants in the international environment. A few constants in the international security environment that spans these four presidents include China, North Korea, Cuba, Israeli-Palestinian conflict, or international terrorism.

Another method to study how the NSSRs were implemented would be to study the subordinate policies of the executive government agencies implementing the NSSRs. This would be relatively easy to study the published *national military strategy* and State Department's strategic plan. A branch off of this study would be to study specifically how the instruments of national power were actually used. What did the State Department, Defense Department, Office of the Foreign Trade Representative actually do?

A branch study off of how these strategies were executed would be a study on how to best implement a national security strategy. It is well recognized that successful policy implementation carries the imperative of close interagency cooperation from all the applicable executive agencies. Since the end of the Cold-War, there are no longer clear distinctions between what is a military task, what constitutes diplomacy, and how all of this overlaps with economic issues. It may make sense to keep separate agencies in Washington, DC where dissimilar opinions are helpful to policy formulation. However, may not make sense to have policy implemented by differing agencies in a particular region. This lack of unity in interagency policy execution has hindered many US government operations, highlighted by the post-conflict phase in Operation Iraqi Freedom.

Another interesting study would be a comparison between what a president says running for office and in the first 100 days compared to what eventually comes out in a NSSR. A variant of this topic would be to compare multiple NSSRs from these four presidents both before and after major international events. For example, what were the changes in the grand strategy of President Reagan after Grenada and Beirut? What were the changes in the grand strategy of President George H. W. Bush after Desert Storm? What were the changes in the grand strategy of President Clinton after Bosnia and Rwanda? What were the changes in the grand strategy of President George W. Bush after invading Iraq (assuming a new national security strategy will be published)?

A final topic for future study ties in with the conclusions of this thesis on the topic of whether the United States needs a true grand strategy or if reacting to crisis is better suited to a democracy. Another way to ask this question is; would national security and US foreign policy be better served with a specific grand strategy, or does the NCS and interagency process work well enough? There are significant historical precedents set for the US where unplanned crisis turn out better for the nation instead of pre-planned strategies.

REFERENCE LIST

Beichman, Arnold. 2002. Providence Abroad. *National Review* 54, no. 1 (28 January): 2.

Brands, H. W. 2001-2002. Four Schoolmasters. *National Interest* no. 66 (winter): 6.

Bush, George H. W. 1990. Remarks Following Discussions with President Mohammed Hosni Mubarak in Cairo, Egypt, 23 November 1990. Available from http://bushlibrary.tamu.edu/papers/1990/90112300.html. Internet. Accessed 4 January 2004.

Bush, George H. W. 1991. *National Security Strategy of the United States*. August 1991. Available from http://www.fas.org/man/docs/918015-nss.htm. Internet. Accessed 20 September 2003.

Bush, George W. 1999. *A Charge to Keep*. New York, NY: William Morrow and Company.

Bush, George W. 2002. *The National Security Strategy of the United States*. 17 September. Available from http://www.whitehouse.gov/nsc/nss.html. Internet. Accessed on 18 April 2003.

Clinton, William J. 1996. *A National Security Strategy of Engagement and Enlargement*. February 1996. Available from http://www.usis.usemb.se/usis/1996strategy/. Internet. Accessed on 5 January 2004.

Department of the Army. 2001. Field Manual 1, *The Army* (14 June). Headquarters, Department of the Army, Washington, DC.

Department of Defense. 2000. Joint Publication 1, *Joint Warfare of the Armed Forces of the United States* (14 November). Joint Chiefs of Staff, Washington, DC.

_____. 2003. Joint Publication 1-02: *DOD Dictionary of Military and Associated Terms* (5 September). Washington, DC: Joint Chiefs of Staff, Washington, DC.

Drew, Dennis M., COL, and Dr. Donald M. Snow. 1988. *Making Strategy: An Introduction to National Security Processes and Problems*. Maxwell Air Force Base, Alabama: Air University Press.

Eccles, Henry E. 1979. *Military Power in a Free Society*. Newport, RI: Naval War College Press.

Book Review (Special Providence). 2002. *Economist* 361, no. 8253 (22 December 2001): 1.

Gaston, James C., ed, 1992. *Grand Strategy and the Decisionmaking Process.* Washington, DC: National Defense University Press.

Hart, Liddell B. H. 1967. *Strategy.* London, England: First Meridian Printing.

International Institute for Strategic Studies (IISS). 2003. International Institute for Strategic Studies Web Page. Available from http://www.iiss.org/aboutiiss.php. Internet.

International Institute for Strategic Studies. 1988. *Strategic Survey: 1987-1988.* London, England: Adlard and Son, Ltd.

_____. 1991. *Strategic Survey: 1990-1991.* London, England: Brassey's.

_____. 1997. *Strategic Survey: 1996-1997.* London, England: Oxford University Press.

_____. 2002. *Strategic Survey: 2001-2002.* London, England: Oxford University Press.

Jordan, Amos A.; William J. Taylor Jr., and Lawrence J. Korb. 1999. *American National Security.* 5th ed. Baltimore, Maryland: Johns Hopkins University Press.

Johns Hopkins University. School of Advanced International Studies. American Foreign Policy Core Requirements, September 2003. Article on-line. Available from www.sais-jhu.edu/programs/afp/afpdeptsyllabi.html. Internet. Accessed on 30 November 2003.

Lord, Carnes. 1988. *The Presidency and the Management of National Security* New York, NY: The Free Press.

Lykke Jr., Arthur F., Colonel US Army, Retired. Defining Military Strategy. 1989. *Military Review* 77 no. 1 (May): 183-186.

Manwaring, Max G., Edwin G. Corr, and Robert H. Dorff. 2003. *The Search for Security: A U.S. Grand Strategy for the Twenty-First Century.* Westport, Connecticut: Praeger.

Mead, Walter Russell. 2001. *Special Providence, American Foreign Policy and How it Changed the World.* New York: Routledge.

Morehead, Philip D. 1995. *The New American Webster Handy College Dictionary.* 3d ed. New York, NY: Penguin Books.

National War College. *Historical Case Studies in Grand Strategy Syllabus.* Document on-line. Available from www.ndu.edu/icaf/departments/gs_mob/3.doc. Internet. Accessed on 30 November 2003.

Nye Jr., Jospeh S. 2003a. U.S. Power and Strategy After Iraq. *Foreign Affairs*. Vol. 82 Issue 4, Jul/Aug2003. 60-73.

_____. 2003b. *Understanding International Conflicts: An Introduction to Theory and History*, 4th Ed. New York, NY: Longman.

_____. 2002. *The Paradox of American Power, Why the World's Only Superpower Can't Go it Alone*. New York: Oxford University Press.

Packard Commission. 1986. *National Security Planning & Budgeting*, President's Blue Ribbon Commission on Defense Management, June 1986. Available from http://www.ndu.edu/library/pbrc/36se2c1.pdf. Internet. Accessed on 18 March 2004.

Reagan, Ronald. 1998. *The National Security Strategy of the United States of the United States*. January. The White House.

Rubin, James P. 2002. Santayana Syndrome. *New Republic* 226, no. 10 (8 March): 374-376.

Sarkesian, Sam C., John Allen Williams, and Steven J. Cimbala. 2002. *U.S. National Security, Policymakers, Processes, and Politics*. Boulder, Colorado: Lynne Rienner Publishers, Inc.

Snider, Don M., and John A. Nagl. 2001. *The National Security Strategy: Documenting Strategic Vision*. Carlisle, Pennsylvania: U.S. Army War College.

Snow, Donald M. 1998. *National Security, Defense Policy in a Changed International Order*. 4th ed., New York: St Martin's Press.

United States Congress. 1947. *The National Security Act of 1947. U.S. Code 50*. 26 July 1947. Available from http://www4.law.cornell.edu/uscode/50/. Internet. Accessed on 2 January 2004.

United States Congress. 1986. *Goldwater-Nichols Defense Reorganization Act of 1986*. 99th Congress, *U.S. Public Law 99-433*. 1 October 1986 http://www.ndu.edu/library/goldnich/goldnich.html. Internet. Accessed on 27 October 2003.

University of California Berkeley. Walter Russell Mead Interview. Conversations with History. *Institute of International Studies*. http://globetrotter.berkeley.edu/ people3/Mead/mead-con0.html. Internet. Accessed on 30 November 2003.

United States Marine Corps. 1997. Marine Corps Doctrinal Publication (MCDP) 1-1, *Strategy*. (November) Headquarters, USMC, Washington DC.

Walton, C. Dale. 2002. Coping with anarchy: Interstate violence and the character of American foreign policy. *Comparative Strategy* 21, no. 5 (October-December): 9.

Yarger, H. Richard, and George F. Barber. 1997. The U.S. Army War College Methodology for Determining Interests and Levels of Intensity. U.S. Army War College Carsile, PA.

Zelikow, Philip. 2001. The United States. *Foreign Affairs*. November/December 2001, *Vol 80, Number 6.* http://www.foreginaffairs.org/ 20011101fabook5791/walter-russell-meade/special-providence-the-secret-strenghts-of-american-foreign-policy.hml Internet. Accessed on 15 January 2004.

INITIAL DISTRIBUTION LIST

Combined Arms Research Library
U.S. Army Command and General Staff College
250 Gibbon Ave.
Fort Leavenworth, KS 66027-2314

Defense Technical Information Center/OCA
825 John J. Kingman Rd., Suite 944
Fort Belvoir, VA 22060-6218

Robert D. Walz, Chair
DJMO
USACGSC
1 Reynolds Ave.
Fort Leavenworth, KS 66027-1352

Brian Allen, First Reader
DJMO
USACGSC
1 Reynolds Ave.
Fort Leavenworth, KS 66027-1352

Stephen D. Coats, Second Reader
DJMO
USACGSC
1 Reynolds Ave.
Fort Leavenworth, KS 66027-1352

CERTIFICATION FOR MMAS DISTRIBUTION STATEMENT

1. Certification Date: 18 June 2004

2. Thesis Author: Major Jeffrey. V. Gardner

3. Thesis Title: Evolving United States Grand Strategy: How Administrations Have Approached the *National Security Strategy Report*

4. Thesis Committee Members: Robert D. Walz, Brian D. Allen, and Stephen D. Coats

Signatures:

5. Distribution Statement: See distribution statements A-X on reverse, then circle appropriate distribution statement letter code below:

(A) B C D E F X   SEE EXPLANATION OF CODES ON REVERSE

If your thesis does not fit into any of the above categories or is classified, you must coordinate with the classified section at CARL.

6. Justification: Justification is required for any distribution other than described in Distribution Statement A. All or part of a thesis may justify distribution limitation. See limitation justification statements 1-10 on reverse, then list, below, the statement(s) that applies (apply) to your thesis and corresponding chapters/sections and pages. Follow sample format shown below:

EXAMPLE

Limitation Justification Statement	/	Chapter/Section	/	Page(s)
Direct Military Support (10)	/	Chapter 3	/	12
Critical Technology (3)	/	Section 4	/	31
Administrative Operational Use (7)	/	Chapter 2	/	13-32

Fill in limitation justification for your thesis below:

Limitation Justification Statement	/	Chapter/Section	/	Page(s)
	/		/	
	/		/	
	/		/	
	/		/	

7. MMAS Thesis Author's Signature: _____